MAX on life
cd-book :: study

Discovering the Power of Prayer

:: 4 Interactive Bible Studies
for Individuals or Small Groups

MAX LUCADO

THOMAS NELSON PUBLISHERS

CONTENTS

HOW TO USE
THIS STUDY GUIDE

Congratulations! You are making God's Word a priority. These moments of reflection will change you forever. Here are a few suggestions for you to get the most out of your individual study.

1

As you begin each study, pray that God will speak to you through His Word.

2

Read the overview to each study, then listen to the audio segment, taking notes on the worksheet provided.

3

Following the audio segment, respond to the personal Bible study and reflection questions. These questions are designed to take you deeper into God's Word and help you focus on God and on the theme of the study.

4

There are three types of questions used in the study. *Observation* questions focus on the basic facts: who, what, when, where, and how. *Interpretation* questions delve into the meaning of the passage. *Application* questions help you get practical: discovering the implications of the text for growing in Christ. These three keys will help you unlock the treasures of Scripture.

5

Write your answers to the questions in the spaces provided or in a personal journal. Writing brings clarity and deeper understanding of yourself and of God's Word.

6

Keep a Bible dictionary handy. Use it to look up any unfamiliar words, names, or places.

7

Have fun! Studying God's Word can bring tremendous rewards to your life. Allow the Holy Spirit to illuminate your mind to the amazing applications each study can have in your daily life. ∎

INTRODUCTION

DISCOVERING THE POWER OF PRAYER

When a believing person prays, great things happen.

JAMES 5:16 NCV

Imagine yourself in a dark room. Windows closed. Curtains drawn. Shutters shut. In the darkness it's hard to believe there's daylight beyond the drapes. So you grope and try to feel your way across the floor. You take a step, disoriented and unsure where you're headed. Progress is slow and the journey painful. Stubbed toes, bruised shins, broken vases. It's hard to walk in a dark place.

Harder still to walk in a dark world. But many try. And, as a result, many are wounded in the effort: tripping over problems, bumping into one another in the shadows, ramming into walls.

But occasionally one of us makes a discovery. Reaching through the blackness, a hand finds curtains and a window latch. "Hey, everybody! The walls have windows!" The drapes are pulled back and the window opened. The sun floods into the room. What was dark is now bright. What was opaque is now clear. What was stale is now fresh.

With the light comes a peace, a power, a desire to move closer to the light, and a confidence to step forward. Our timid steps are replaced by a certainty to our walk. A certainty to move through the corridors of life, opening one window after another to illuminate. What a difference! And all it took was one small gesture of opening curtains and raising the window.

Prayer does the same thing for us. Prayer is the window that God has placed in the walls of our world. Leave it shut and the world is a cold, dark house. But throw back the curtains and see His light. Open the window and hear His voice. Open the window of prayer and invoke the presence of God in your world.

That's what this study, *Discovering the Power of Prayer*, is all about. ■

*More things are wrought
by prayer than this world dreams of.*

ALFRED, LORD TENNYSON

LESSON ONE:

THE LIFELONG CHANCE OF A LIFETIME

This is the confidence we have in approaching God: that if we ask anything according to his will, he hears us.

1 JOHN 5:14 NIV

OVERVIEW

Most of our prayer lives could use a tune-up. Some prayer lives lack consistency. They're either a desert or an oasis. Long arid, dry spells interrupted by brief plunges into the waters of communion. . . .

Others of us need sincerity. Our prayers are a bit hollow, memorized and rigid. More liturgy than life. And though they are daily, they are dull.

Still others lack, well, honesty. We honestly wonder if prayer makes a difference. Why on earth would God in heaven want to talk to me? If God knows all, who am I to tell Him anything? If God controls all, who am I to do anything?

Our prayers may be awkward. Our attempts may be feeble. But since the power of prayer is in the One who hears it and not the one who says it, our prayers do make a difference.

I experienced a kindred truth many years ago. My daughters and I spent a Saturday desk-hunting. I needed a new one for the office, and we'd promised Andrea and Sara desks for their rooms. Sara was especially enthused. When she comes home from school, guess what she does? She plays school! I never did that as a kid. I tried to forget the classroom activities, not rehearse them. My wife, Denalyn, assures me not to worry, that this is one of those attention-span differences between genders. So off to the furniture store we went.

When Denalyn buys furniture, she prefers one of two extremes—so antique it's fragile or so new it's unpainted. This time we opted for the latter and entered a store of in-the-buff furniture.

Andrea and Sara succeeded quickly in making their selections, and I set out to do the same. Somewhere in the process Sara learned we weren't taking the desks home that day, and this news disturbed her deeply. I explained that the piece had to be painted and they would deliver the desk in about four weeks. I might as well have said four millennia.

Her eyes filled with tears. "But, Daddy, I wanted to take it home today."

Much to her credit, she didn't stomp her feet and demand her way. She did, however, set out on an urgent course to change her father's mind. Every time I turned a corner she was waiting on me.

"Daddy, don't you think we could paint it ourselves?"

"Daddy, I just want to draw some pictures on my new desk."

"Daddy, please let's take it home today."

After a bit she disappeared, only to return, arms open wide and bubbling with a discovery. "Guess what, Daddy. It'll fit in the back of the car!"

You and I know that a seven-year-old has no clue what will or won't fit in a vehicle, but the fact that she had measured the trunk with her arms softened my heart. The clincher, though, was the name she called me: "Daddy, can't we please take it home?"

The Lucado family took a desk home that day.

I heard Sara's request for the same reason God hears ours. Her desire was for her own good. What dad wouldn't want his child to spend more time writing and drawing? Sara wanted what I wanted for her, she only wanted it sooner. When we agree with what God wants, He hears us, as well (1 John 5:14).

Sara's request was heartfelt. God, too, is moved by our sincerity. The "earnest prayer of a righteous man has great power" (James 5:16 TLB).

But most of all, I was moved to respond because Sara called me "Daddy." Because she is my child, I heard her request. Because we are His children, God hears ours. The King of creation gives special heed to the voice of His family. He is not only willing to hear us, but He loves to hear us when we come to Him.

It doesn't matter how old you are or what problems you are facing in your life. You have been given the lifelong chance of a lifetime: to come before the God of the universe, to approach Him in all of His power and glory, and to be received as His child, His precious son or daughter whom He loves with all of His heart.

Prayer: It's the lifelong opportunity of a lifetime. Let's get started on learning how to make the most of it!

PART 1:
FOLLOW-ALONG NOTES

USE THIS WORKSHEET AS YOU LISTEN TO "DISCOVERING THE POWER OF PRAYER, PART 1."

· Once every twenty-five years, the pope and some priests demolish a wall to get into a room in St. Peter's Cathedral. What if that's how prayer was? What if we were only allowed to approach God every twenty-five years?

· Ephesians 2:18 - Access

· We have access to our _____.

· We have access through _____ _____.

· We are empowered by the _____ _____.

- You have _____ to the throne of God.

- Your Father wants to hear from you.

- You matter to God.

- _____ tries to say your prayers do not matter.

- Abba Father

PART 2:
GOING DEEPER

PERSONAL STUDY AND REFLECTION

God listens intently and carefully to your prayers. Your prayers are honored as precious jewels to Him. Purified and empowered, the words rise in a delightful fragrance to our Lord.

· Write out Revelation 8:4 on the lines below.

_____

_____

_____

· How did the prayers of God's people rise up to His throne in heaven?

_____

_____

_____

Incredible! Your words do not stop until they reach the very throne of God. One call and heaven's fleet appears. Your prayer on earth activates God's power in heaven.

- According to James 5:13, who should pray?

_____

_____

_____

_____

- Why is prayer important? (List as many ways as you can think of.)

_____

_____

_____

_____

· Write out James 5:16 on the lines below.

_____

_____

_____

_____

· What is the effect of a righteous person's prayers?

_____

_____

_____

_____

Your prayers move God to change the world! You may not understand the mystery of prayer. You don't need to. But this much is clear: Actions in heaven begin when someone prays on earth. What an amazing thought!

· Have you ever considered the fact that your prayers could change the world? In what ways does your world need to be changed? How could you begin to pray for those changes to take place?

_____

_____

_____

Although my daughters are growing up fast, I hope they never get to the point where they are too grown up to call their daddy. That's how God feels about you! He always wants you to call on Him, no matter what situations you are facing.

· What hinders you from praying with confidence?

_____

_____

_____

· What can you do to let go of those hindrances and begin to pray with the confidence of a true child of God?

_____

_____

_____

· What situation or person will you pray for in faith this week? To begin, write out a simple prayer to the Lord on the lines below and then believe that He has heard your prayer—and will answer.

_____

_____

_____

When you speak, Jesus hears.

And when Jesus hears, the world is changed. ■

I have found the perfect antidote
for my fears and problems.
Whenever they stick up their ugly faces,
I just clobber them with prayer.

DALE EVANS ROGERS

LESSON TWO:

WHEN DOING ALL YOU DO ISN'T ENOUGH

Trust in him at all times,
O people; pour out your hearts
to him, for God is our refuge.

PSALM 62:8 NIV

OVERVIEW

If God had a refrigerator, your picture would be on it. If He had a wallet, your photo would be in it. He sends you flowers every spring and a new sunrise every morning. Whenever you want to talk, He'll listen. He can live anywhere in the universe, and He chose your heart. And the Christmas gift He sent you in Bethlehem? Face it, friend. He's crazy about you!

And because he loves you, he wants to hear from you. Prayer allows you to communicate with the heart of a God who loves you so very much. Your voice matters in heaven. God takes you and your concerns seriously. When you enter His presence, He turns to hear your voice. No need to fear that you will be ignored. Even if you stammer or stumble, even if what you have to say impresses no one, it impresses God. He listens to the painful plea of the elderly in the rest home. He listens to the gruff confession of the death-row inmate. When the alcoholic begs for mercy, when the spouse seeks guidance, when the businessman steps off the street into the chapel, God listens.

Intently. Carefully.

Not only does God listen, but He has the power to help. I can remember as a youngster knowing some kids whose fathers were quite successful. One was a judge. The other a prominent physician. I attended church with the son of the mayor. In Andrews, Texas, that's not much to boast about. Nevertheless the kid had clout that most of us didn't. "My father has an office at the courthouse," he could claim.

Guess what you can claim? "My Father rules the universe."

What controls you doesn't control God. What troubles you doesn't trouble Him. What fatigues you doesn't fatigue Him. Is an eagle disturbed by traffic? No, he rises above it. Is the whale perturbed by a hurricane? Of course not, he plunges beneath it. Is the lion flustered by the mouse standing directly in his way? No, he steps over it.

How much more is God able to soar above, plunge beneath, and step over the troubles of the earth! "With man this is impossible, but with God all things are possible" (Matthew 19:26 NIV). The God who created the heavens is able to answer your prayers, and His resources are available to help you deal with your problems—even when they are bigger than you are.

How vital it is to pray, armed with the knowledge of God's power and willingness to help in your time of need!

PART 1:
FOLLOW-ALONG NOTES

USE THIS WORKSHEET AS YOU LISTEN TO "DISCOVERING THE POWER OF PRAYER, PART 2."

- What power source do you rely on?

- Zachariah 4:6

- We can do nothing until we pray.

- All Christians have been given the same power source in prayer.

- Ephesians 2:19

I. When should you pray?

When the _____ is greater than you are.

Acts 12

II. How should you pray?

As if your _____ depended upon it.

James 5:16

III. Why should you pray?

So that the Lord _____.

So that the Lord _____.

So that the Lord _____.

PART 2:
GOING DEEPER

PERSONAL STUDY AND REFLECTION

· How do you tend to react in trying times? (Be honest!)

_____

_____

_____

· _What controls you doesn't control God. What troubles you doesn't trouble Him. What fatigues you doesn't fatigue Him._

What earthly concerns currently control, trouble, or fatigue you? Check all that apply.

❏ Relationship struggles

❏ Stock market

❏ Monthly bills

❏ Illness

❏ Crime or violence in the world

❏ Work

- *When faced with such concerns, we need God's perspective in order to trust that He is in control and to pray with confidence.*

Which of the following statements are true about God's perspective on our problems, and which ones are false? Mark your answers True (T) or False (F). Use the Bible verses provided to help you answer.

____ The resources of heaven belong to God to deal with our problems. (Psalm 115:16).

____ Our heavenly Father knows exactly what we need. (Matthew 6:32)

____God is not interested in listening to our concerns. (Psalm 65:2).

____What limitations control us on earth do not control Him in heaven. (Psalm 103:11).

- *God does not always answer our prayer in the ways that we expect, but He always answers—and He always acts toward us in the way that would benefit us the most.*

Consider a recent concern you have brought to God in prayer. Are you expecting God to work along human lines (what you think should be done) or are you asking for His higher ways?

_____

_____

_____

_____

_____

_____

_____

_____

Read Ephesians 3:20. Fill in the blanks below about what you learn concerning God meeting your needs.

· With _____ power working in _____,

God can do much _____ than anything we can

_____ or _____.

If God is able to place the stars in their sockets and suspend the sky like a curtain, do you think it remotely possible that God is able to guide your life? If your God is mighty enough to ignite the sun, could it be that He is mighty enough to light your path? If He cares enough about the planet Saturn to give it rings or Venus to make it sparkle, is there an outside chance that He cares enough about you to meet your needs? ∎

*Prayer does not equip us
for greater works—prayer
is the greater work.*

OSWALD CHAMBERS

LESSON THREE:

PRAYER—THE SECRET STRENGTH

But he said to me, "My grace is enough for you.
When you are weak, my power is made perfect in you."
So I am very happy to brag about my weaknesses.
Then Christ's power can live in me.

2 Corinthians 12:9–10 ncv

OVERVIEW

We are tempted to wait to pray until we know how to pray. We've heard the prayers of the spiritually mature. We've read of the rigors of the disciplined. And we are convinced we've a long way to traverse.

And since we'd rather not pray than pray poorly, we don't pray. Or we pray infrequently. We are waiting to pray until we learn how to pray.

But the honest prayers of hurting people reach the very heart of God and provide the strength to make it through. God is moved more by our pain than by our eloquence. And He responds. That's what fathers do.

That's exactly what Jim Redmond did too.

His son, Derek, a twenty-six-year-old Briton, was favored to win the four-hundred-meter race in the 1992 Barcelona Olympics. Halfway into his semifinal heat, a fiery pain seared through his right leg. He crumpled to the track with a torn hamstring.

As the medical attendants were approaching, Redmond fought to his feet. "It was an animal instinct," he would later say. He set out hopping, pushing away the coaches in a crazed attempt to finish the race.

When he reached the stretch, a big man pushed through the crowd. He was wearing a T-shirt that read, "Have you hugged your child today?" and a hat that challenged, "Just Do It." The man was Jim Redmond, Derek's father.

"You don't have to do this," he told his weeping son.

"Yes, I do," Derek declared.

"Well, then," said Jim, "we're going to finish this together."

And they did. Jim wrapped Derek's arm around his shoulder and helped him hobble to the finish line. Fighting off security men, the son's head sometimes buried in the father's shoulder, they stayed in Derek's lane to the end.

The crowd clapped, then stood, then cheered, and then wept as the father and son finished the race.

What made the father do it? What made the father leave the stands to meet his son on the track? Was it the strength of his child? No, it was the pain of his child. His son was hurt and fighting to complete the race. So the father came to help him finish.

God does the same. Our prayers may be awkward. Our attempts may be feeble. But since the power of prayer is in the One who hears it and not the one who says it, our prayers do make a difference.

PART 1:
FOLLOW-ALONG NOTES

USE THIS WORKSHEET AS YOU LISTEN TO "DISCOVERING THE POWER OF PRAYER, PART 3."

- Exodus 17:8-15

- Where was the decisive battle fought?

- They learned from their answered prayers to _____ _____.

- Remember how the battle was won.

- The question: If God is in control, why do my prayers matter?

- Revelation 3:20 is written to believers.

- We are _____ in a dark world.

- God's window is _____.

- The purpose of prayer: _____

  _____.

- There is never a time when communion with God should cease.

PART 2:
GOING DEEPER

PERSONAL STUDY AND REFLECTION

- Which of the following statements are true concerning the power of prayer, and which ones are false? Mark your answers True (T) or False (F).

____ We must pray just the right prayer to get Jesus to help us.

____ Jesus only answers the prayers of the super-spiritual.

____ The power we need is in Jesus, not in our prayers.

- Read the following verses. Then match the verse with what you learn about how God's power stacks up against our own.

____ Psalm 20:7

____ Psalm 29:4

____ Jeremiah 10:12

____ Mark 1:7

____ Hebrews 1:3

a. He holds everything together in His power.

b. God created the earth by His power.

c. Trusting in God is better than trusting in others.

d. The Lord's voice alone is powerful.

e. Jesus is greater than the most "spiritual" person.

- Despite our inconsistencies on a daily basis, a crisis often drives our prayers to the height of sincerity and honesty. We know we need help! Look up the following verses below and write down what you learn about acknowledging our neediness.

- 1 Samuel 1:10–11

_____

_____

_____

_____

- Psalm 17:1

_____

_____

_____

_____

_____

- Romans 7:24

_____

_____

_____

_____

· What does Matthew 17:20 teach you about how Jesus stressed the connection between belief and power?

_____

_____

_____

Our need puts Jesus into action. It sounds the alarm! It catches His ear. Why? Because He loves us.

· Read Isaiah 40:11 and answer the following questions:

What imagery is used to describe God's tender strength?

_____

_____

_____

How does He respond to weakness?

_____

_____

_____

_____

_____

In what areas of your life do you find it difficult to believe and trust in God? What areas are difficult to approach God with in prayer?

_____

_____

_____

_____

What "impossible" task can you assault with your prayer of faith this week?

*Prayer is not overcoming
God's reluctance; it is laying hold
of His highest willingness.*

R. C. TRENCH

LESSON FOUR:

LED BY AN UNSEEN HAND

I love the Lord, for he heard my voice;
he heard my cry for mercy.
Because he turned his ear to me,
I will call on him as long as I live.

PSALM 116:1–2 NIV

OVERVIEW

Certain things about God are easy to imagine. I can imagine Him creating the world and suspending the stars. I can envision Him as almighty, all-powerful, and in control. I can fathom a God who knows me, who made me, and I can even fathom a God who hears me. But a God who is in love with me? A God who is crazy for me? A God who cheers for me?

But that is the message of the Bible. Our Father is relentlessly in pursuit of His children. He has called us home with His Word, paved the path with His blood, and is longing for our arrival.

God's love for His children is the message of the Bible.

I read recently about a man who had reached the end of his life. A few days before he died, a priest went to visit him in the hospital. As the priest entered the room, he noticed an empty chair beside the man's bed. The priest asked him if someone had been by to visit. The old man smiled, "I place Jesus on that chair, and I talk to Him."

The priest was puzzled, so the man explained. "Years ago a friend told me that prayer was as simple as talking to a good friend. So every day I pull up a chair, invite Jesus to sit, and we have a good talk."

Some days later, the daughter of this man came to the parish house to inform the priest that her father had died. "Because he seemed so content," she said, "I left him in his room alone for a couple of hours. When I got back to the room, I found him dead. I noticed a strange thing, though: His head was resting, not on the pillow, but on an empty chair that was beside his bed."[1]

The heart of your Father longs for you to spend time in His abiding presence. Why don't you pull up a chair and join Him?

[1] Walter Burkhardt, *Tell the Next Generation* (Ramsey, NJ: Paulist, 1982) 80, quoted in Brennan Manning, *Lion and Lamb* (Old Tappan, NJ: Chosen, Revell, 1986), 129. This illustration was pulled from *Experiencing the Heart of Jesus*.

PART 1:
FOLLOW-ALONG NOTES

USE THIS WORKSHEET AS YOU LISTEN TO "DISCOVERING THE POWER OF PRAYER, PART 4."

- We often choose to try to make it on our own instead of seeking God's help or allowing Him to "fill us with gas."

- 2 Chronicles 7:14

- Is it possible to pray without ceasing? Is it possible to continually offer praises to God?

1 Thessalonians 5:17

Ephesians 6:18

Philippians 4:6

Luke 18:1

Romans 12:12

Colossians 4:2

Hebrews 13:15

- We must invite God into our presence.

- Results of more time in God's presence:

_____

_____

_____

_____

- James 4:8

- Heaven is looking for someone to speak.

PART 2:
GOING DEEPER

PERSONAL STUDY AND REFLECTION

· What role did prayer play in your family's life when you were growing up? How did this help or hinder your acceptance of God's love for you?

_____

_____

_____

_____

_____

_____

· Read the following verses. Then match the verse with what you learn about God's care and concern for you.

    ___ Psalm 10:14

    ___ Psalm 34:15

    ___ Psalm 46:1

    ___ Isaiah 41:10

    a. *He always helps in times of trouble.*

    b. *He will make us strong and support us.*

    c. *He listens to our prayers.*

    d. *He helps us when we feel like orphans.*

· Read Psalm 59:16–17 and fill in the blanks regarding how much God loves you and wants to spend time with you.

In the morning, we can _____ about God's _____.

He is our defender and place of _____ in times of

_____. We can sing _____ about Him. He

is the God who _____ us.

· According to 1 Thessalonians 5:17, we are to "pray without ceasing." What does it mean to you to pray continually in this manner?

_____

_____

_____

_____

· If God already knows what we need before we ask, why do you think is it still so important to pray continually?

_____

_____

_____

_____

- What changes are you planning on making to your prayer life as a result of this study? Write out your plan, and then commit to making it happen in your life!

_____

_____

_____

_____

_____ ■

PROMISES FROM DISCOVERING THE POWER OF PRAYER

Savor the following promises that God gives to those who determine to discover the power of prayer in their lives. One way that you can carry the message of this study with you everywhere in your heart is through the lost art of Scripture memorization. Select a few of the verses below to commit to memory.

When a believing person prays, great things happen.

JAMES 5:16B NCV

Jesus looked at them and said, "With man this is impossible, but with God all things are possible."

MATTHEW 19:26 NIV

God is our protection and our strength. He always helps in times of trouble.

PSALM 46:1 NCV

[Jesus said,]
"If you remain in me and my words remain in you,
ask whatever you wish, and it will be given you."

JOHN 15:7 NIV

[Jesus said,]
"Ask and it will be given to you; seek and you will find; knock and
the door will be opened to you. For everyone who asks receives;
he who seeks finds; and to him who knocks, the door will be opened."

MATTHEW 7:7–8 NIV

The LORD sees the good people and listens to their prayers.

PSALM 34:15 NCV

And this is the boldness we have in God's presence: that if we ask God
for anything that agrees with what he wants, he hears us. If we know he
hears us every time we ask him, we know we have what we ask from him.

1 JOHN 5:14–15 NCV

With God's power working in us, God can do much,
much more than anything we can ask or imagine.

EPHESIANS 3:20 NCV ■

SUGGESTIONS FOR MEMBERS OF A GROUP STUDY

The Bible says that we should not forsake the assembling of ourselves together (see Hebrews 10:25). A small-group Bible study is one of the best ways to grow in your faith. As you meet together with other people, you will discover new truths about God's Word and challenge one another to greater levels of faith. The following are suggestions for you to get the most out of a small-group study of this material.

1. Come to the study prepared. Follow the suggestions for individual study mentioned previously. You will find that careful preparation will greatly enrich your time spent in group discussion.

2. Be willing to participate in the discussion. The leader of your group will not be lecturing. Instead, he or she will be encouraging the members of the group to discuss what they have learned. The leader will be asking the questions that are found in this guide.

3. Stick to the topic being discussed.

4. Be sensitive to the other members of the group. Listen attentively when they describe what they have learned. You may be surprised by their insights! Many questions do not have "right" answers, particularly questions that aim at meaning or application. Instead the questions push us to explore the passage more thoroughly.

5. When possible, link what you say to the comments of others. Also be affirming whenever you can. This will encourage some of the more hesitant members of the group to participate.

6. Expect God to teach you through the passage being discussed and through the other members of the group. Pray that you will have an enjoyable and profitable time together, but also that as a result of this study, you will find ways that you can take action individually and/or as a group.

7. Remember that anything said in the group is considered confidential and should not be discussed outside the group unless specific permission is given to do so. ■

LEADER'S GUIDE

1. Begin the session with prayer. Ask God to be with you as you begin to study His Word together.

2. Play the audio segment of the CD entitled "Discovering the Power of Prayer, Part 1." Encourage group members to take notes in the section of their study guide entitled "Follow-Along Notes."

3. Begin group discussion by asking the following questions. Allow each group member ample time to answer, if they desire to do so.

   - What first comes to your mind when you hear the word *prayer*?

   - What role has prayer played in your own personal walk with God?

   - Has there ever been a time when prayer and/or spending time with God was difficult for you? Why or why not?

- What hinders you from praying with confidence? What can you do to let go of those hindrances and begin to pray with the confidence of a true child of God?

- Read James 5:16 together as a group. What results do you desire to see when you pray?

4. Remind everyone to complete the "Going Deeper: Personal Study and Reflection" section for lesson two before the next group session.

5. Be sure to close in prayer. Invite the group participants to share prayer requests with the group and encourage them to pray for one another.

L E S S O N   T W O :   W H E N   D O I N G   A L L   Y O U   D O   I S N ' T   E N O U G H

1. Begin the session with prayer. Ask God to be with you as you begin to study His Word together.

2. Play the audio segment of the CD entitled "Discovering the Power of Prayer, Part 2." Encourage group members to take notes in the section of their study guide entitled "Follow-Along Notes."

3. Begin group discussion by asking the following questions. Allow each group member ample time to answer, if they desire to do so.

   • How do you tend to react in trying times? What happens to your prayer life when you encounter difficult circumstances? (Be honest!)

   • Describe a time when one of your prayers was answered. How can the reminder of this time help to build your faith in God today?

   • Read Ephesians 3:20 as a group. What do you expect God to do for you? How might He meet or exceed your expectations?

- "God does not always answer our prayers in the ways that we expect, but He always answers—and He always acts toward us in the way that would benefit us the most." Do you agree with this statement? Why or why not?

4. Remind everyone to complete the "Going Deeper: Personal Study and Reflection" section for lesson three before the next group session.

5. Be sure to close in prayer. Invite the group participants to share prayer requests with the group and encourage them to pray for one another.

LESSON THREE: PRAYER—THE SECRET STRENGTH

1. Begin the session with prayer. Ask God to be with you as you begin to study His Word together.

2. Play the audio segment of the CD entitled "Discovering the Power of Prayer, Part 3." Encourage group members to take notes in the section of their study guide entitled "Follow-Along Notes."

3. Begin group discussion by asking the following questions. Allow each group member ample time to answer, if they desire to do so.

   - What keeps you personally from praying?

   - How easy or difficult is it for you to consider God as a loving Father, willing to give good gifts to His children? What has shaped your attitude and beliefs in this regard?

   - In what areas of your life do you find it difficult to believe and trust in God? What areas are difficult for you to bring to God in prayer? Why?

• How can you begin to turn these areas over to the Lord and trust Him to care for you in every aspect of your life?

4. Remind everyone to complete the "Going Deeper: Personal Study and Reflection" section for lesson four before the next group session.

5. Be sure to close in prayer. Invite the group participants to share prayer requests with the group and encourage them to pray for one another.

LESSON FOUR: LED BY AN UNSEEN HAND

1. Begin the session with prayer. Ask God to be with you as you begin to study His Word together.

2. Play the audio segment of the CD entitled "Discovering the Power of Prayer, Part 4." Encourage group members to take notes in the section of their study guide entitled "Follow-Along Notes."

3. Begin group discussion by asking the following questions. Allow each group member ample time to answer, if they desire to do so.

   - Has there ever been a time in your life when you knew *about* God without really *knowing Him* and experiencing His love firsthand? If so, how has your life changed since that time?

   - Is it really possible to "pray without ceasing"? If so, how?

   - What is the difference between the words "God, let me do a great thing for You" and "God, do a great thing through me"? Which prayer do you usually pray? Why? What are the results?

- How can you begin to "pull up a chair for Jesus" and spend time in His constant, abiding presence every day? What is your plan? Ask your fellow group members to encourage you to put your plan into action in the upcoming days and weeks.

4. Be sure to close in prayer. Invite the group participants to share prayer requests with the group and encourage them to pray for one another. ∎

MAX LUCADO'S

MAX on life

S E R I E S

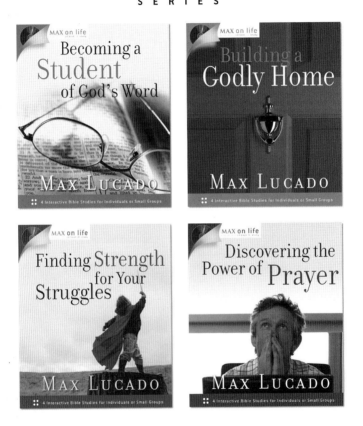

AVAILABLE WHEREVER BOOKS ARE SOLD.